THE ISLAND OF
HAWAI'I

**FERNS COMING UP THROUGH
LAVA CRACKS IN HAWAI'I
VOLCANOES NATIONAL PARK**

THE ISLAND OF
HAWAI'I

RAINBOW FALLS, HILO

KEAWAIKI, KOHALA COAST

THE ISLAND OF
HAWAI'I

Mutual Publishing

Photography by **Douglas Peebles**

Text by **Jan TenBruggencate**

Mutual
Publishing

Library of Congress
Catalog Card Number 2001117031

Book Design
Michael Horton Design

ISBN-10: 1-56647-500-7
ISBN-13: 978-1-56647-500-6

First Printing, October 2001
Second Printing, October 2004
Third Printing, September 2007
Fourth Printing, May 2009
Fifth Printing, December 2010

Mutual Publishing
1215 Center Street, Suite 210
Honolulu, Hawaii 96816
Telephone (808) 732-1709
Fax (808) 734-4094
Email: info@mutualpublishing.com
www.mutualpublishing.com

Printed in China

TABLE OF CONTENTS

LAPAKAHI STATE PARK

THE ISLAND OF HAWAIʻI

KEAWAIKI

ʻŌHIʻA LEHUA FLOWER

is different. What I like most about going there is that I never know what I am going to find. It is always changing. It is, of course, the only island still growing. Lava is pouring out of the vents or into the ocean most every day. I always enjoy going to Hawaiʻi Volcanoes National Park to watch that process, especially at twilight.

Hawaiʻi is also the island that changes the most throughout the year. Snow comes and goes from Mauna Kea and Mauna Loa during the winter. Kāhili ginger and other flowers take over the roadsides at different times. Hilo and the Hāmākua coast can be stunningly blue or completely gray from one day to the next. Both are beautiful to see. The views in Waimea and Kohala can change even faster as the trade winds blow swiftly over the mountains.

All of this creates both challenge and opportunity for a photographer. I love it, and while Hawaiʻi may not be the easiest island to shoot, it is the most interesting. If you don't get what you want the first time, you can always go back to the same spot again. It will be different.

Douglas Peebles

ANTHURIUM

IN THE BROADEST SENSE

FOREWORD

of the term, Hawai'i could be viewed as a pu'uhonua, a place of refuge, where people in old Hawai'i were protected from dangers, freed from pursuit. The highest places on this vast island stand out when approaching the Islands from the south or the east, tantalizing testimony to the presence of a place of safety from the vagaries of wind and wave. Its highest mountains rise above the cloud line, appearing to float on the mists. The missionary William Ellis, in his "Polynesian Researches," describes this phenomenon about the island of Hawai'i.

"It is the most southern of the whole, and, on account of its great elevation, is usually the first land seen from vessels approaching the Sandwich Islands. Its broad base and regular form render its outline different from that of any other island in the Pacific with which we are acquainted."

The island's mountains are referred to as shield volcanoes, having developed in a form that is broad like a warrior's shield rather than into steep-sided cones. Ellis said they "do not pierce the clouds like obelisks or spires, but in most parts, and from the southern shore in particular, the ascent is gradual, and comparatively unbroken, from the sea-beach to the lofty summit of Mouna Roa [Mauna Loa]."

CHANTING AT SUNSET
WAIKOLOA

For early visitors, arriving at the Islands after weeks or months at sea, the appearance of land in such a surreal form sometimes took on an appearance of fantasy.

"The elevated summit of Mouna Kea, or Mouna Roa, has appeared above the mass of clouds that usually skirt the horizon, like a stately pyramid, or the silvered dome of a magnificent temple, distinguished, from the clouds beneath, only by its well-defined outline, unchanging position, and the intensity of brilliancy occasioned by the reflection of the sun's rays from the surface of the snow."

ORCHID

Some authors have suggested that this must have been the first island the first Polynesians spotted due to the prominence of these mountains from a vast distance. Others have added that the relentless pressure of the trade winds would have pushed early voyagers westward, to an eventual landing on the leeward islands. Indeed, some of the earliest archaeological dates in the Islands are from coastal sites on Moloka'i and O'ahu. Studies of language and artifacts on Kaua'i and Ni'ihau also suggest these leeward islands have an older link to the rest of Polynesia than the windward islands of the Hawaiian chain.

PU'U 'Ō'Ō VENT

But because of the high visibility, the mountains of Hawai'i island would have quickly drawn visits from the earliest settlers. On arriving at the shores of Hawai'i's volcanoes, they would have found there one of the largest islands in all of Polynesia. A refuge, or pu'uhonua, from the sea. The native historian Samuel Manaiakalani Kamakau said a pu'uhonua could be the person of a chief or chiefess to whom one could run for protection, a temple where defeated warriors could gain safety, or a district.

HAWAIIAN CEREMONY AT KILAUEA CALDERA

"The concept of pu'uhonua came down from ancient times, and pu'uhonua lands had always been observed. They were sacrosanct and inviolable lands; no blood of wrongdoers could be shed once they entered into these pu'uhonua lands," Kamakau wrote.

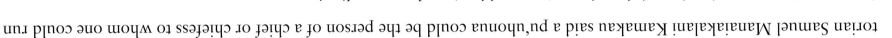

In the earliest days, there were few people, and according to some accounts no chiefs and no wars. To settlers from overcrowded, combative islands to the south, it must have seemed like a puʻuhonua indeed.

That changed with increasing population, the establishment of a rigid caste system of priests and chiefs, commoners and outcasts. Battles over resources and power became common, and the chiefs of Hawaiʻi developed into some of the most powerful of warlords. Kamehameha was the ultimate. He adopted Western firepower in the form of cannons and muskets, and wove them into traditional fighting systems to create an unstoppable war machine.

But with the Western guns that allowed Kamehameha to unite the Islands came other changes. Cattle were allowed to roam the lands, and soon large tracts of upland property were turned over to ranches. Native

KOA FOREST ON SLOPE
OF MAUNA KEA

forests where Hawaiians collected logs for canoes, birds for feather capes and plants for medicine were converted to pasture. Sugar cultivation, started on Kaua'i in 1835, spread into the fertile lowlands, sometimes replacing Hawaiian agricultural properties. A native Hawaiian community devastated by disease, its population down from hundreds of thousands to a few tens of thousands, could not work the vast agricultur-

RAINFOREST, HAWAI'I
VOLCANOES NATIONAL PARK

al fields, so immigrants were imported, primarily from Asia and Europe, changing the faces of the islands. A century later, tourism began moving into the beach areas, developing hotels and golf courses, access roads and support communities. In the last few decades, the highest mountaintops, the ones spotted by the earliest sailors, were converted to scientific enclaves, where astronomers puzzle out the origins of the universe. Thus was the Island of Hawai'i changed, from its reefs to its highest rocks.

The state of Hawai'i has been called a melting pot, a term used to represent the blending of the ethnic groups. The Island of Hawai' today is indeed a complex stew, blending its volcanic heritage with the spices of all the changes humans have brought. And while it has changed dramatically, there still exists evidence of many of its past lives. There are undeveloped coastlines, preserved archaeological remains of early Hawaiian fishing villages, quaint plantation camps and upscale resort subdivisions. Vegetation ranges from native forest within national parks to mixed stands of alien and Hawaiian plants in lowland valleys, from macadamia-nut orchards to coffee fields to banana plantations to pots of flowers growing in volcanic cinder under shadecloth shelters. The people of this island come from every point on the globe, each attracted for his or her own reason to Ellis' "silvered domes." Each ethnic group has brought change to the island, and has been changed by the island.

WATERFALLS IN
WAIMANU VALLEY

One is inescapably changed by this island. It is, after all, alive. Earth tremors are frequent occurrences. Volcanic eruptions are common. And on the wide southeastern shore, lava flows regularly add to the island's acreage. The pu'uhonua is growing.

KOHALA SUNSET

OUTRIGGER
CANOE

HILO/HĀMĀKUA

THE CITY OF HILO

is known for its rain and its profusion of vegetation. The rich volcanic soil supports plants of every description, and many species grow luxuriant with their roots pushing down into solid rock. In recorded history, it has always been so. When the traveler Isabella Bird visited more than a century ago, she wrote:

"I cannot convey to you any idea of the greenness and lavish luxuriance of this place, where everything flourishes, and glorious trailers and parasitic ferns hide all unsightly objects out of sight. It presents a bewildering maze of lilies, roses, fuchsias, clematis, begonias, convolvuli, the huge granda, the purple and yellow water lemons, also custard apples, rose apples, mangoes, mangostein, guavas, bananas, breadfruit, magnolias, geraniums, candlenut, gardenias, dracaenas, eucalyptus, pandanus, ōhias, kamani trees, kalo, noni, and quantities of other trees and flowers, of which I shall eventually learn the names, patches of pineapple, melons, and sugar cane for children to suck, and sweet potatoes."

ANTHURIUM

KAMEHAMEHA DAY
CELEBRATION, HILO

Her list includes so many introduced plants that it seems almost anything brought to Hilo sprouted and thrived. Sugar cane became the main industry of this place, and while this grass did well here, the cloud cover associated with Hilo's wet climate limited the production. Sunnier areas grew cane better and cheaper.

The state government tried to convert Hilo into a major visitor destination area, but like the cane, tourists prefer sunnier coasts. With the decline of sugar cane, Hilo has developed into a service town, with headquarters offices for astro-

HULA AT HILO FESTIVAL

nomical observatories that sit atop Mauna Kea, the jumping-off point for trips to Kīlauea Volcano, a four-year college and the seat of county government. Its tsunami museum recalls the catastrophic ocean waves that destroyed its waterfront, which has now been converted into a sprawling park. Up the Hilo slopes is the Lyman House Museum, which tells some of the island's history.

The windward coast that leads northwest from Hilo to Honoka'a is called the Hāmākua Coast. Once full of sugar fields, many of them tilled by independent growers, its plantation towns are now quiet hamlets, their sugar mills gone silent. Many of the towns have become quaint spots where tourists stop to acquire handicrafts, woodwork, art and a sense of the island's history. The old cane fields grow timbertree crops, macadamia nuts, papayas and cattle.

Visitors stop at the Hawai'i Tropical Botanical Gardens and swing through the artsy village of Honomū on the way to stunning 'Akaka Falls. The heavy rains that water this coastline have cut deep, jagged valleys, and drivers cross bridge after bridge. The coast swings in and out of scenic bays and rocky points. Waterfalls abound. The Kolekole Beach Park, between Honomū and Hakalau, is worth a visit.

The Hāmākua Coast is steeped in Hawaiian history. At Laupāhoehoe, Kamehameha, still in the process of conquering the island chain, fought famous battles with the forces of the Big Island chief Keawemauhili. Kamehameha attacked with three armed forces: an army of bowmen, an army of expert sling throwers, and the one he personally led, a third army of warriors expert in the use of battle-axes and spears. By the end of the second battle, which lasted three full days, some of Keawemauhili's soldiers are reported to have thrown themselves over sea cliffs to avoid further conflict

MERRIE MONARCH FESTIVAL

with the fierce Kamehameha forces. These actions presaged similar suicidal leaps by Oʻahu warriors faced by Kamehameha's armies at Nuʻuanu.

At Laupāhoehoe today, the train museum recalls the days when locomotives hauled sugar cane and people up and down the coast. At the Laupāhoehoe shore, a small park and a memorial commemorate the tsunami that wiped out much of a generation of this town when it swept into the school.

A long drive inland between Paʻauilo and Honokaʻa takes you to Kalōpā State Park, a nature-lover's mountain paradise set in an old ʻōhiʻa forest.

The road eventually reaches Honokaʻa, a fascinating blend of old sugar town and older cow town, with touches added by each immigrant population. The Katsu Goto Memorial speaks of the Japanese influence, and the malasadas served at Tex Drive-In add a Portuguese flavor.

WAIPI'O VALLEY

VALLEY ALONG HĀMĀKUA COAST
NEAR HILO

WAIPIʻO

ANTHURIUMS READY FOR MARKET

WAIPI‘O VALLEY

'AKAKA FALLS

WAIĀKEA POND, HILO

HILO WITH MAUNA KEA IN BACKGROUND

PLANTATION TOWN ALONG HĀMĀKUA COAST

HĀMĀKUA COAST
Previous pages

KOA TREE ON THE SLOPES OF MAUNA KEA WITH
MAUNA LOA IN THE BACKGROUND

KALO FIELD, WAIPI'O VALLEY

WATERFALL IN WAIMANU VALLEY

HĀMĀKUA COAST

SLOPES OF MAUNA KEA

HORSESHOEING IN WAIPI'O VALLEY

ONO AT SUISAN FISH MARKET, HILO

Chapter Two

WAIMEA
COWBOY COUNTRY

THE PLAINS OF WAIMEA

sprawl at an elevation around 3,000 feet between the southern end of the old, weather-beaten Kohala Mountains and the broad slopes rising to Mauna Kea. The central town for this region has two names: Waimea and Kamuela. One story accounting for this phenomenon is that the proper name is Waimea, but that an early postmaster's name, Samuel or Kamuela, was often used to direct mail to the area. Another suggestion is that Kamuela was not the postmaster, but a prominent resident whose name became associated with the region. Still another story is that Kamuela is named for Samuel Parker, a grandson of the founder of Parker Ranch. Some folks will tell you that the name of the town is Waimea, but that the name of the Waimea post office is Kamuela.

This is a region whose economy is in the midst of change from its two-century-old cowboy heritage to a cool, upland retirement community with touches of other economies. It houses the headquarters for the Canada-France-Hawai'i telescope and the twin Keck telescopes, whose observatories are atop Mauna Kea. And it is home to two respected private schools, Hawaii Preparatory Academy and Parker School. The region is also known for its agriculture. Some of the best fresh vegetables are grown in these upland fields, where many varieties do better than in the hotter lowlands.

PARKER RANCH

ALOHA WEEK PARADE, WAIMEA

Still, it is difficult to avoid the reminders of The Ranch. Waimea's Parker Ranch is one of the oldest in Hawai'i. It is the largest ranch in Hawai'i. Rodeos are frequent occurrences in the region. And the cow-town theme is a popular one in stores and restaurants.

But before there were cows, the area was forest and plain with active populations of native Hawaiians. Waimea was known in those times for its chill wind, the Kīpu'upu'u. The warriors of the district were considered particularly strong in battle, but they were also used as messengers, since they were reputed to run as fast as the wind blew in their district. They were strong supporters of Kamehameha in his battles to unite the districts of the Big Island and then the other islands under unified rule. Kamehameha named his army of Waimea warriors the Kīpu'upu'u. A Waimea forest called Mahiki was a source of many of the spears used by Kamehameha's armies in battles.

PARKER RANCH

Cattle had been protected from hunting by a royal kapu after their introduction to the Islands by Capt. Vancouver. They roamed the countryside in increasing numbers. Kamehameha issued to John Palmer Parker, a sailor who jumped ship in the Islands, the first permit to hunt the wild cattle. Parker marketed them as salt beef, hides and tallow, and they became a significant export. Parker established his headquarters at Waimea. His ranch grew through purchases and vast leases to become the largest ranch under single ownership in the nation, covering some

225,000 acres. It was run by or for Parker's heirs until the death of Richard Smart, who left it to a charitable trust to support the Waimea community.

While Waimea is becoming more and more of a bedroom community, its history is well preserved in several locations. The Parker Ranch Visitor Center has the Parker Museum, a walk-through museum that tells the story of the ranch and of cattle with photographs and artifacts of the ranch's history. There are tours available of historic ranch homes. The Kamuela Museum is a private museum with wonderful collections of Hawaiian artifacts, as well as a Parker family descendant's personal collections from around the world. 'Imiola Church, built of koa in 1857, dates to a time when early Christians were actively recruiting Hawaiians into the church, and the churches were central to community life.

'IMIOLA CHURCH, WAIMEA

KAHUĀ RANCH, WAIMEA

40   **KOHALA MOUNTAINS**
Previous pages

WAIKI'I RANCH

ALOHA WEEK PARADE, WAIMEA

STRAWBERRY FARM, WAIMEA

PARKER RANCH

PU'UHUE RANCH

WAIMEA
Previous pages

THE OLD KOHALA

KOHALA

mountain range at the northern end of the Big Island is the result of volcanic activity of one of five volcanoes still visible on the island. The others are Mauna Kea, Mauna Loa, Kīlauea and Hualālai. A sixth, called Māhukona, has been completely covered by the lavas of later volcanoes. Kohala's highest peak reaches a little more than a mile high. Kohala is very different from much of the rest of the island. Its age has allowed the forces of erosion to wear it down. Its east coast is a steep land of narrow valleys and high ridges where no roads have been built. The west coast is the stark land where the Hawaiian archipelago's first king, Kamehameha, was born and raised.

TI PLANT

Kamehameha would have been born in a less remote part of the island except for extraordinary measures taken to protect him at birth. His mother was at the royal court of Alapa'i in Hilo when that chief became concerned that the unborn child would be a threat. There had been signs that were interpreted as meaning that the youngster would be a killer of chiefs. The pregnant chiefess was taken into hiding in North Kohala, where her child grew up and was trained in the skills of a warrior.

The king's birthplace, now a stone enclosure along a dirt road leading south from the tiny 'Upolu Airport, provides broad views of the sea. From here, the grassy fields rise gently to the Kohala ridge. A short distance north lies the ancient Mo'okini heiau, a powerful place of human sacrifice and a national historic landmark.

KAPALOA FALLS ALONG
KOHALA DITCH TRAIL

KAHUĀ RANCH

It was a rich land. Missionaries report that as they traveled through the region in the 1820s and 1830s, the residents brought them large quantities of food, including chickens, turkeys, ducks, fish and pigs. There were taro, banana, breadfruit, sugarcane, and baked sweet potato, all washed down with calabashes of fresh water.

Kohala is an isolated part of the island, protected from aggressive development in part by its distance from major airfields and by its challenges of access. While roads run up the region's western coast and wrap around the northern point near ʻUpolu, only very difficult foot trails push in from either end into the east-facing section between Pololū Valley and Waipiʻo Valley.

The windward section of the Kohala Mountains is so rugged that while it is all technically part of Kohala, Waipiʻo is more closely linked to the Hāmākua District. The roads leading to the rim of Waipiʻo extend from Honokaʻa in Hāmākua, not from anywhere in Kohala. It is so rugged that in the early days, much of this coast was preferably traversed by canoe rather than on foot.

MOʻOKINI HEIAU

One remarkable feat of engineering during the early stages of the sugar industry was the construction of extensive ditch systems along impossibly steep terrain. The Kohala Ditch is one of these, and the Kohala Ditch Trail, which allowed plantation ditch workers access for maintenance, snakes in and out of valleys for a dozen miles as the crow flies, and far more on the ground. Much of it is now in poor repair.

MAKAĪWA BAY

KAPALOA FALLS

The water from this ditch system and the Kehena Ditch fed the lush sugar fields of the Kohala Sugar Company, but in the early 1970s the plantation closed. North Kohala's frequent overcast skies limited sugar yields, and its isolation increased transportation costs, and the company could not make money. That left cattle as the main use of much of the Kohala land. Today, small towns in the Kohala Mountains are quiet, rustic villages best known for their art shops, catering mainly to tourists.

The region is full of historical sites. The Lapakahi State Historical Park is a restored Hawaiian fishing village. Some of the finest snorkeling to be found in the Islands is offshore, at the Koai'e Cove Underwater Park, a state marine-life conservation district.

In the village of Kapaʻau stands the original Kamehameha statue, a tall sculpture which shows the great chief with one arm extended, looking out over his country. It recalls the words Kamehameha is said to have uttered on his deathbed: "Endless is the good I have conquered for you."

KAHUĀ RANCH

'ANAEHO'OMALU BAY

SUNSET AT MAUNA LANI, MAKAĪWA BAY

ROUTE 250 BETWEEN WAIMEA AND HĀWĪ

COCONUT PALMS AT KEAWAIKI BEACH

KEAWAIKI BEACH
Previous pages

HĀPUNA BEACH STATE PARK

ANCHIALINE POND

PUAKŌ PETROGLYPHS

AERIAL VIEW OF MAUNA LANI RESORT

KŪKIʻO BEACH, KAʻŪPŪLEHU

MOʻOKINI HEIAU

KAUNAʻOA BEACH AT MAUNA KEA RESORT

GOING SURFING AT HUALĀLAI
FOUR SEASONS RESORT

CARVED COCONUT-PALM STUMP

18TH HOLE, HUALĀLAI RESORT

KONA

THE TRADE WINDS BLOWING from the northeast over the great mountains of Mauna Kea and Mauna Loa create a lee on the western side of the island, an area of low rainfall, light wind, calm water and sunny skies. If there is a single downside to the splendid conditions of the Kona Coast, it is that fumes from volcanic eruptions at Kīlauea are often trapped here, creating a persistent volcanic fog, called vog. Distant sights tend as a result to be slightly obscured by a kind of surreal mistiness. Even this has its upside. Kona's sunsets, already spectacular over the clear horizon, are enhanced by the light filtering through the vog.

KING
KAMEHAMEHA
CELEBRATION

SAINT BENEDICT'S
PAINTED CHURCH

This is the Big Island's playland. Outrigger canoes ply the tropical waters. Charter fishing boats head out with the dawn, chasing after the big tunas and marlins for which these waters are famous. Surfers ride a few reef breaks when a swell from the west rises up. Snorkelers find wonders throughout the coastline, locating coral growing directly on the black lava-rock substrate. Kahaluʻu Beach Park and Kealakekua Underwater State Park are prime spots. Cruise ships anchor offshore, bringing visitors ashore in small boats to wander the town of Kailua's historic waterfront and visit the shops and restaurants.

To the north, developers have carved green oases out of the black, arid lava lands of South Kohala, setting hotels on the rare sandy beaches and inserting championship golf courses among the vast slabs of pāhoehoe lava, some of which

IRONMAN TRIATHALON FINISH LINE

display carved images, called petroglyphs, left by earlier visitors—many of the petroglyphs date to pre-contact times and may represent a form of communication that has never been satisfactorily translated. The ancient Hawaiian foot trail through the region is marked by a worn smooth surface on the rough lava, indicating how much the trail was used.

To the south of Kailua are a few bays marked with resort hotels and condominium projects, but farther along, the rocky coast goes local. At Hōnaunau Bay there was in early Hawaiian times a place where those fleeing the law could find refuge. According to tradition, a criminal or someone politically out of favor was safe from harm if he or she could reach the pu'uhonua here. The area is now pre-

SPINNER DOLPHIN OFF KONA

served as the Pu'uhonua O Hōnaunau National Historical Park, better known as the City of Refuge.

Small bays and headlands farther south are occupied by tiny villages, or individual guest houses, or campgrounds visited by residents who arrive by boat or by four-wheel-drive cars over rough lava roads. The best known of the little communities south of Kailua is Miloli'i, an ancient fishing village where the anglers still use outrigger canoes. Today, the canoes are built of planks rather than dugout logs. They are painted bright colors and they are often powered by outboard motors.

Inland, the Kona coast rises quickly up the slopes of the island's volcanoes. To the north, South Kohala lies primarily on the slopes of Mauna Kea, and South Kona on the slopes of Mauna Loa. The land mauka of Kailua rises to the 8,271-foot peak of Hualālai.

The cooler, wetter upland areas have a very different character from the coastlines. South Kohala's uplands tend to be dry, but are used for pasture. South Kona's uplands, noted as among the island's most productive koa-logging regions, are also pasture areas. Today, there are extensive natural reserves in both places, aimed at protecting the native vegetation and wildlife of the region.

KEALAKEKUA FRUIT STAND

In between, the uplands of North Kona are commonly known as Hawai'i's coffee country. The region has dozens of small family coffee farms, where the flowers in the spring turn the fields white, and the red cherries are picked in the fall. Most are processed locally, producing the world-renowned Kona coffee. The villages of the coffee country provide plenty of opportunity to buy coffee, either from large commercial roasters or individual farms. Coffee shops are plentiful. So are small art shops, a sign that the coffee country has also attracted artisans who work in a range of media—painting, carving, pottery, sculpture, fine furniture and lots more.

CAPTAIN COOK MONUMENT,
KEALAKEKUA BAY

KAILUA-KONA

CHURCH IN MILOLI'I

UCHIDA COFFEE FARM

HUALĀLAI SUMMIT

HULIHE'E PALACE

FISH AND POI

FISHING CANOES AT HOʻOKENA BEACH

KONA SUNSET

PU'UHONUA O HŌNAUNAU

THE VAST STRETCH

KA'Ū/PUNA VOLCANO COUNTRY

NĒNĒ GEESE

from Ka Lae or South Point to Cape Kumukahi encompasses the entire southeastern side of the Big Island. Lava flows into the sea midway along this coast. The region includes the Hawai'i Volcanoes National Park and is one of the least populated sections of Hawai'i Island. The district of Ka'ū lies to the south and Puna to the north. In ancient mythology, these were districts that belonged to the fire goddess, Pele. In legend, as in reality, the volcano constantly confronts the vegetated parts of the island. Hawaiian history says the volcano lands were Pele's, while the forested country belonged to her male rival, Kamapua'a.

At South Point, one of the most consistently windy places in the Islands, windmills stand like ancient giants, their arms endlessly swinging. On the coast, the wind and water sweeping down the east coast of the island meet the protected waters of the leeward side at Ka Lae, where the island's shore makes a sharp right-hand turn. At the confluence of these waters is a rich fishing ground in deep water near the shore. For early Hawaiian fishermen, launching canoes on this rocky coast was difficult, and holding position over the best fishing spots was difficult, so they developed a unique technique. They kept their canoes tethered to the shore on long ropes. Presumably, this way a canoe wasn't blown far offshore while the paddlers were hauling their catch aboard.

HAWAIIAN CEREMONY
AT KĪLAUEA CALDERA

Today, dozens of the canoe mooring rings carved into the shoreline rock are still visible. In modern times, anglers have launched skiffs off derricks built out over the edge of the cliffs. Outboard motors make it easier to hold a boat's position, and the mooring rings are no longer used.

The quiet town of Nāʻālehu is the village that lies nearest the southernmost point of the island. The writer Mark Twain, while visiting the Islands in 1866, is said to have planted a monkeypod tree in nearby Waiʻōhinu. The tree blew down nearly 100 years later, but it is said to have been replanted using material from the original, and the descendant tree can be viewed today. Twain liked the area, and referred to it without his normal caustic wit: "In this rainy spot trees and flowers flourish luxuriantly and three of those trees—two mangoes and an orange—will live in my memory as the greenest, freshest, and most beautiful I ever saw—and withal, the stateliest and most graceful." Twain had just come off a very rough sea voyage, and may simply have been thrilled to be on land.

The writer went by mule up the long slope to the summit of Kīlauea, and noted the changing countryside: "We came upon a long dreary desert of black, swollen, twisted, corrugated billows of lava—blank and dismal desolation!" Later he would describe with eloquence the view of the boiling lava lake at Halemaʻumaʻu, seen at night.

GEOLOGIST TAKING A MEASUREMENT
FROM A SKYLIGHT

KĪLAUEA LAVA FLOWS INTO THE OCEAN

Much of the Kīlauea region is now preserved as a national park, and is far more accessible than in Twain's time. The author stayed at the Volcano House, and the modern successor of that simple resort still stands on the rim of the Kīlauea crater. Mules, however, are no longer required for access to the wonderland that some have called the world's only drive-in volcano. Hawai'i's volcanoes, though there are

PĀHOEHOE LAVA

exceptions, tend to go quietly about the business of building islands. While they can have stunning fountains, major explosions are comparatively rare. Numerous trails, maintained by the National Park Service, take active visitors to a range of sights, from great beds of lava to walk-through volcanic tubes and tree molds, where lava has encircled trees in the forest and then burned them up, leaving their shapes behind.

Much of the park is covered in native forest, and one of the jobs of the park service is to fight off invading alien plants and animals that threaten the native ecosystems here.

Visitors to the volcano in recent years have had the added benefit, unavailable to Twain, of being able to see the island grow before their eyes. During the two decades of Kīlauea's latest eruption, mostly from its East Rift Zone vent at Puʻu ʻŌʻō, it has more or less continuously flowed to the sea. When conditions are right, visitors can hike across the

PUNALUʻU HARBOR AND BLACK-SAND BEACH

lava to the steaming, hissing, glowing area where the lava exits its protected underground tube and pours out onto the shore.

East of the summit is the district of Puna. Most of Kīlauea's lava flows have repeatedly cut through the southern part of Puna on flows to the sea. The village of Kalapana was completely destroyed by lava in the 1980s, just as much of the village of Kapoho to the north was wiped out two decades earlier. But the lava is a rich base for vegetation, and parts of the Puna region are dense in native forest. Many of the island's flower farms—specializing in anthuriums, orchids and heliconias—are situated in this region. A number of huge rural subdivisions have also been created here, with roads bulldozed through the ʻōhiʻa forest. Residents get large lots at low prices, but many also suffer limited government service, since some of the developments were built without provision for municipal water, power or government-standard roads.

PUNALU‘U BLACK-SAND BEACH

HAWAIIAN CEREMONY AT KĪLAUEA CALDERA

ʻŌHIʻA LEHUA TREE NEAR SULFUR VENT

SULFUR DEPOSITS ON UWĒKAHUNA BLUFF

KAPOHO BAY

GREEN-SAND BEACH, SOUTH POINT

KĪLAUEA LAVA FLOW

CINDER CONE, PUʻU ʻŌʻŌ

KĪLAUEA LAVA FLOWS INTO THE OCEAN

PU'U 'Ō'Ō FOUNTAIN

LAVA TUBE SKYLIGHT

LAVA FLOWS INTO THE OCEAN

LAVA FLOWS INTO THE OCEAN

SOUTH POINT LOOKING TOWARDS MILOLI'I

WINDMILLS AT SOUTH POINT

HAWAI'I VOLCANOES NATIONAL PARK

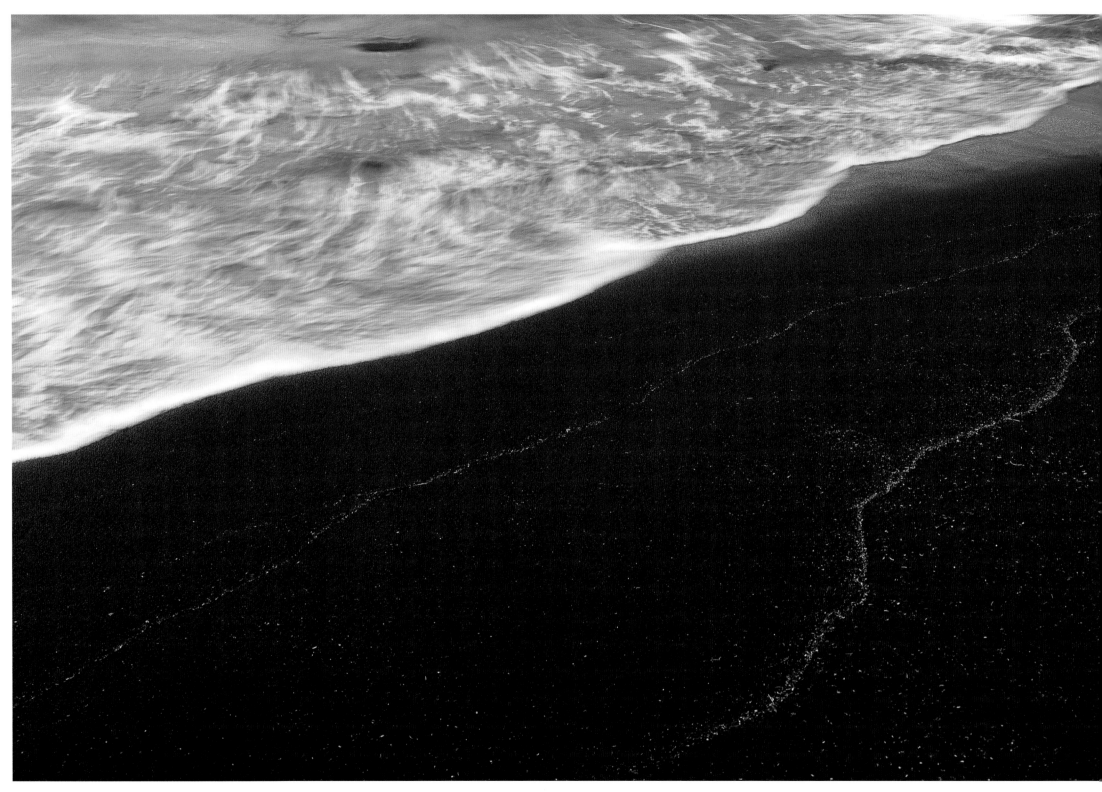

HAWKSBILL TURTLE ON PUNALU'U BEACH

LAVA FLOWS INTO THE OCEAN

HAWAIIAN VOLCANO OBSERVATORY
AND HALEMAʻUMAʻU CRATER

MAUNA KEA
MAUNA LOA

THE TOP MILE OF

the Big Island belongs to the two great mountains, Mauna Kea and Mauna Loa. Kīlauea's peak at Uwēkahuna attains 4,090 feet. The highest point in the Kohala Mountains exceeds a mile high at 5,480 feet. Hualālai tops out half a mile higher at 8,271 feet. But beyond that, a full mile in vertical elevation, the island is entirely within the realm of the two great mountains, both of which easily pierce the 13,000-foot level.

Mauna Kea, the higher peak at 13,796 feet, is much more accessible thanks to its value to the astronomy community, which has developed a road to the village of telescopes at its summit. The state's government is attempting to balance the often competing requirements of astronomers, native Hawaiians and naturalists for the mountaintop.

Astronomers say Mauna Kea's peak is perhaps the best place on the face of the planet for this kind of work. The peak is higher than much of the Earth's atmosphere, providing clearer views. Its paved road provides great access. The University of Hawai'i's Institute for Astronomy runs a mid-level facility at about 9,000 feet in elevation, providing scientists a place to work and rest between trips to the summit, where cold temperatures and thin air can create problems.

But it offends some residents that the observatories are visible at the peak from many parts of the island, like a cluster of white golf balls marring the otherwise natural appearance of the great volcano. Those concerned about Hawaiian cultural remains on the peak, which include stone heiau, or temples, say the construction activity and traffic threatens the archaeological remains, both physically and in their spiritual integrity.

Naturalists point out that despite the appearance of lifelessness at the peak, which is made up of cinder cones and lava flows, a highly specialized ecosystem has developed. It includes insect species that contain a kind of antifreeze in their

MAUNA KEA WITH MAUNA LOA IN THE BACKGROUND

KAUNALOA BEACH WITH
MAUNA KEA IN BACKGROUND

tissues, allowing them to survive freezing temperatures. Environmental groups argue that both astronomy and the tourist traffic generated as a result of the summit road threaten these life forms.

Early Hawaiian use of the mountain was varied. Besides the religious and cultural uses suggested by heiau on the mountain, an extremely dense lava flow below the summit was mined for tools. The Mauna Kea adz quarry is considered one of the two or three best sources of stone in the entire archipelago. Birds were collected here for their feathers, which were used in capes, helmets and other decorative applications. Larger birds were also collected here for their meat.

Both Mauna Kea and Mauna Loa are often covered with snow in winter. Ski enthusiasts wait for infrequent good snow cover and arrive at the Mauna Kea summit for a few runs down the powdered cinder slopes. The stunning views across the island and across the ʻAlenuihāhā Channel to Maui's Haleakalā provide a breathtaking experience. So does the thin air at this elevation.

Mauna Loa's 13,677-foot height is attained only on foot, generally via either of two arduous trails up its east slope. It is the larger of the two mountains in volume, calculated at 19,000 cubic miles. While Mauna Kea rises to a peak, Mauna Loa is topped with a summit caldera, a great depression caused when magma drained from under the peak, causing it to collapse. Kīlauea has a similar caldera, nearly as large. (Magma is the name geologists give to molten rock when it is still underground. When it erupts, it is renamed lava.)

While Mauna Kea has been inactive for perhaps thousands of years, Mauna Loa remains an active volcano. It erupts briefly every decade or so.

HUALĀLAI WITH MAUNA KEA AND MAUNA LOA IN THE BACKGROUND

Slung between the two great peaks is an area residents call The Saddle, where the lavas from Mauna Kea and Mauna Loa meet, one lapping over the other. A rough road between Hilo and Waimea, the Saddle Road, is off-limits under most rental-car contracts. The road has a narrow shoulder and sharp turns, and in most areas has no place to pull off in case of trouble.

The Army runs a military training area over a vast chunk of this country, called the Pōhakuloa Training Area. Some call the region the Humuʻula Saddle, using the Hawaiian place name for acreage that in the last century was used as a sheep station. Cattle now run on the the old sheep pastures.

AERIAL OF MAUNA KEA

CALTECH SUBMILLIMETER OBSERVATORY ON MAUNA KEA

MAUNA LOA

THE ISLAND OF HAWAI'I—SITE DESCRIPTIONS

Page i Ferns, whose spores are scattered by the winds across new lava, spring up in a crack at Hawai'i Volcanoes National Park. They are often the first visible forms of life to appear on new lava flows.

Page iii In a classic tourist poster shot, Rainbow Falls in Hilo is framed in the huge leaves of monstera and lit with the orange blossoms of African tulip.

Pages iv/v KEAWAIKI AREA

Page vii LAPAKAHI STATE PARK

Page 1 PALM ON BLACK-SAND BEACH

Page 1 The bright red starburst shape of the lehua blossom is a familiar sight in Hawai'i forests, but the leaves of the plants can come in various shapes and sizes, and some are covered with fine white hairs. The flowers, too, are variable, and varieties in orange and yellow colors are sometimes found.

Page 2 A native Hawaiian chanter, dressed in flowing robes, a floral headpiece and a lei of the fragrant alyxia vine maile gestures to the setting sun at Waikoloa.

Page 2 ANTHURIUM

Page 3 ORCHID

Page 4 Reaching for the sky, hula dancers perform an ancient hula at the edge of the firepit in Kīlauea Caldera, as visitors look on from behind rope barriers.

Page 4 The dense steam and acrid smoke rising from the Pu'u 'Ō'ō vent atop Kīlauea's East Rift Zone creates a volcanic smog or vog that is a health hazard to Hawai'i residents with respiratory problems.

Page 5 The lava glows yellow and orange as it flows into the ocean amid clouds of steam during an eruption of Kīlauea.

Page 6 Tree ferns shade the undergrowth under an open canopy of primarily 'ōhi'a trees within Hawai'i Volcanoes National Park.

Page 7 Landslides, earthquakes, and constant erosion by wind and water have cut plunging cliffs along the back of Waimanu Valley, which lies along the roadless coastline from Waipi'o to Pololū Valleys, where streams drain northeast from the main ridge of the Kohala Mountains.

Pages 8/9 Jagged lava creates calm bays and quiet inlets, seen here in a sunset scene at Mauna Lani resort's Makaīwa Bay.

Page 10 Two men watch an outrigger canoe on the sands of Hilo Bayfront Park.

Page 10 Not just the old red heart shape any more. Anthurium breeders have taken their industry into a range of new territories with commercial-quality blooms, new shapes, colors and sizes.

Page 10 Helmets worn by Hawaiian royalty, built on a light framework of 'ie'ie aerial roots and covered with bird feathers, are seen today in events like Hilo's King Kamehameha celebration.

Page 11 Dancers festooned in green raise their hands to the heavens at a hula festival in Hilo.

Page 12 Hula dancers display colorful lei at the Merrie Monarch Festival. Begun in 1946, the Festival honors the memory of King David Kalākaua, who, during his reign, restored many Hawaiian traditions and festivals that had been prohibited by missionaries in the early 19th century. Since its first year, the Merrie Monarch has become a premiere hula competition and a much anticipated event for spectators.

Page 13 Located near the University of Hawai'i-Hilo campus, the 'Imiloa Astronomy Center provides visitors with a link to Hawai'i's ancient past as well as its future. Exhibits at the center include those concerning ancient Hawaiian methods of navigating by the stars, natural history exhibits about the island, and demonstrations of current research being conducted at Mauna Kea.

Pages 14 A bird's-eye view of Waipi'o Valley.

Page 15 The heavy rainfall along the Hāmākua Coast and the rich volcanic soil join in supporting dense tropical vegetation. These slopes were once cloaked in native vegetation, but most of the plants in this photograph, including the palms, are introduced.

Page 16 The wide, firm sand of the beach at Waipi'o, with its backdrop of stark green cliffs, provides a scenic spot for a horseback ride.

Page 17 Fresh bunches of anthuriums ready for sale at the Hilo open market.

Page 18 A cottage and a famous waterfall form a classic photo of Waipi'o Valley.

Page 19 'Akaka Falls, plunging in a straight drop of 442 feet, is one of the premier visitor attractions along the Hāmākua Coast north of Hilo. It is a state park lying along Kolekole Stream mauka of the village of Honomū.

Page 20 Ancient, spreading trees and an old Japanese-style footbridge stand along Hilo's Waiākea Pond, which draws its water from an upland stream of the same name and flows into Hilo Bay as the Wailoa River.

Page 21 Hilo is a green town, well-watered by the trade-wind rains. The Waiākea Pond in the foreground flows into Hilo Bay.

Pages 22/23 The heavy rainfall along the Hāmākua Coast and the rich volcanic soil join in supporting dense tropical vegetation. These slopes were once cloaked in native vegetation, but most of the plants in this photograph, including the palms, are introduced.

Page 24 Sugar is gone now, but the many small plantation towns along the rugged Hāmākua Coast remain, some of them nestled up against the edges of the cliffs, with wide views of the ocean to the east.

Page 25 An ancient koa tree, a remnant of when these slopes of Mauna Kea were densely forested, stands starkly against Mauna Loa in the background. Trees like this one, often more than a century old, date to before cattle ranching fully converted the forests to grassland.

Page 26 A grower harvesting taro holds up a championship sample in a taro patch in Waipi'o Valley.

Page 27 A waterfall cascades into Waimanu Valley. The sparse vegetation on both sides of the falls clings to minimal soil on cliffs mostly made of basalt. Many of the darkest green trees are ʻōhiʻa. The palest trees to the right of the falls are kukui. The light green between the trees represents patches of the false staghorn fern, uluhe.

Pages 28/29 A rain-swollen waterfall along the Hāmākua Coast.

Pages 30/31 Ancient Hawaiian forest trees, covered in lichen, stand out against the background sky.

Page 32 Horses aren't much used in Hawaiʻi any longer for transportation, but in the most rural regions, such as remote Waipiʻo Valley, shoeing horses is still a valued skill.

Page 33 One of the prized eating fish in Hawaiʻi is the ono, known on the mainland as wahoo. Here, a good morning's catch is on display at Suisan, the fish market along the Wailoa River in Hilo.

Page 34 The stunning kāhili ginger is fragrant and colorful, but it is a noxious weed in the Hawaiian forest, where it forms dense clumps that exclude native plants. The kāhili, unlike its relatives, the yellow and white flowering gingers, produces seeds in Hawaiʻi which are quickly spread through the forest.

Page 34 A pair of horses, enjoying freedom from bits and saddles, spends a quiet sunset on the upland pastures of Parker Ranch, near Waimea.

Page 35 The cowboy traditions of Waimea are evident at parade time, when it seems half the town is on horseback. Here, riders participate in Waimea's Aloha Week parade.

Page 36 When Charlie Kimura retired as a cowboy at Parker Ranch, he ended three generations of Kimuras who rode the Waimea pastures on horseback.

Page 37 The sun turns the grassy hills golden behind historic ʻImiola Congregational Church on Church Row in Waimea.

Pages 38/39 High on the slopes of the Kohala Mountains, the green pastures of Kahuā Ranch sport wildflowers.

Pages 40/41 Cinder cones in the background betray the volcanic origin of this pastureland in the Kohala Mountains, on Kahuā Ranch.

Page 42 Waikiʻi Ranch, along the Saddle Road on the northwestern slope of Mauna Kea, is nearly a mile above sea level. The upland mists frequently drift through the pastures, keeping its grasses watered.

Page 43 A pāʻū rider and her horse, resplendent in flowers, accept cheers from the crowd during the annual Aloha Week parade in Waimea.

Page 44 Truck crops thrive in the Waimea uplands. Here, a grower displays a harvest of fresh strawberries.

Page 45 Ancient, twisted kiawe fenceposts mark the pasture boundaries separating horses from cattle in this scene on Parker Ranch, with the slopes of Mauna Kea rising in the background.

Pages 46/47 The uplands of Waimea, where good soil, cool temperatures and a friendly fog meet and some of Hawaiʻi's finest vegetables are grown.

Pages 48/49 Curious cattle inspect the photographer in a pasture at North Kohala's Puʻuhue Ranch.

Page 50 A variegated ti plant, displaying rich pinks and greens, on display at a Hawaiʻi Island botanical garden.

Page 50 The original statue of King Kamehameha at Kapaʻau in North Kohala was placed in the king's home district after being recovered from the waters of the Falkland Islands, where it had gone down with the ship carrying it from Europe to Hawaiʻi. The identical statue in Honolulu is a replica. Similar statues also stand in Hilo and Washington.

Page 50 Kapaloa Falls on the Kohala Ditch Trail.

Page 51 Low clouds hang ominously over horses grazing in a Kahuā Ranch pasture. Clouds form a regular part of the scene on these fields high in the Kohala Mountains.

Page 51 A traditional thatched house stands within the Moʻokini Heiau, a major temple that was reported to have been a luakini, or temple where human sacrifice was performed.

Page 52 Visitors walk on a lava rock shelf, inspecting the shorebreak along Makaīwa Bay at the Mauna Lani Resort.

Page 52 Hikers take photos and prepare to pass under the Kapaloa Falls on the Kohala Ditch Trail, which was built to provide ditch maintenance workers access to the streams, waterfalls, ditches and tunnels of the old sugar irrigation system.

Page 53 A tree standing tall against the ever-present winds at Kahuā Ranch points some of its branches to leeward.

Pages 54/55 ʻANAEHOʻOMALU BAY

Page 56 Coconut palms planted close together stretch in all directions to get their share of sunlight, their fronds exploding outward like dark fireworks, seen here against the sunset at Makaīwa Bay, Mauna Lani.

Page 57 The ironwood tree-lined Kohala Mountain Road, state highway 250, runs between pastures on the southern slopes of the Kohala Mountains, between Waimea and the northern town of Hāwī.

Pages 58/59 The black sand, made of volcanic rock fragments, is speckled with bits of white coral washed up from the sea at Keawaiki Beach.

Pages 60/61 KEAWAIKI BEACH-COCONUT PALMS

Page 62 Just another day in Hawaiʻi. White-sand beaches are not common on the Big Island, but Hāpuna Beach State Park's strand is one of the best in the state, with waters normally warm, calm and clean.

Page 63 Anchialine Ponds are inland pools that form in ancient lava depressions and tubes. The pools are connected to the ocean and the water tends to be rather salty. In Hawaiʻi, it is common to find ʻōpae (shrimp) living in the waters of an anchialine pond.

Page 64 Hawaiian rock carvings, or petroglyphs, take many forms, including animals, humans, canoes and abstract figures whose meaning remains unknown. Here, at Puakō, the largest image in the foreground is a stick figure of a man.

Page 65 The Mauna Lani Resort is celebrated for its luxury accommodations, golf courses, and lush surroundings. It has recently become renowned for its commitment to the environment—most of its electricity is generated through solar power and the resort has begun an ecotourism program to educate visitors about local flora and fauna.

Pages 66/67 A shaded beach, a protected coastal swimming pond and an outrigger canoe present a classic Hawaiian scene at Kūki'o Bay at Ka'ūpūlehu.

Page 68 The Mo'okini Heiau, on a windy hill in North Kohala not far from the birthplace of Kamehameha, is associated with Pa'ao, a Tahitian priest who transformed Hawaiian society. It is a national landmark.

Page 69 The visitors lying on beach mats and towels are barely visible in this view of stunning Kauna'oa Beach at the Mauna Kea Resort.

Page 70 A surfer with a colorful board passes the shaded beach chairs fronting the Four Seasons Resort at Hualālai, north of Keāhole.

Page 71 A comparatively modern tradition is to take a coconut tree and turn it roots-up to create the appearance of wild hair over a carved face.

Pages 72/73 The sand traps appear to be formed by cookie cutters on the green fairways of Hualālai's 18th hole.

Pages 74/75 WAIKOLOA SUNSET

Page 76 An active charter fishing fleet operates in the usually calm waters off Kailua. Here, a fishing boat heads out on a charter.

Page 76 An island princess rides on horseback in Kona's King Kamehameha celebration, wearing seed and flower lei and a spiked floral headpiece.

Page 76 St. Benedict's Catholic Church, better known as The Painted Church of Hōnaunau, built in 1875, was given its remarkable interior artwork between 1899 and 1904 by Father John Velge.

Page 77 The Big Island's Kona Coast is famous for many things, but one of the events that gets the most international publicity is the Ironman Triathlon. The finish of the original swim-bike-run endurance event is seen here.

Page 77 Schools of spinner dolphin often come into shallow coastal areas, apparently to enjoy themselves. Here, a dolphin performs in waters off Kona.

Page 78 A fruit stand in Kealakekua displays both imported crops and mangoes and papayas picked from trees in the neighborhood.

Page 78 Kayakers often bring their colorful craft to the spot where a monument has been placed in memory of Capt. James Cook, the English navigator who first visited the Islands in 1778 and who died here, on the shores of Kealakekua Bay.

Page 79 A cruise ship stands offshore while smaller pleasure craft anchor closer in at the Kailua coastline, often referred to as Kona or Kailua-Kona.

Page 80 The humble church in the village of Miloli'i seems to fit the quiet fishing village it oversees.

Page 81 Cherries of most coffee varieties are ripe when they're red. Kona coffee cherries are hand-picked at peak ripeness, and the seeds, or coffee beans, are removed to be dried, roasted, brewed and enjoyed.

Page 81 A basket of mostly ripe coffee cherries displayed at the Uchida coffee farm.

Page 82 The summit of Hualālai, at 8,271 feet above sea level, is the third-highest peak on the Big Island, but is dwarfed by Mauna Kea and Mauna Loa.

Page 83 Hulihe'e Palace in Kailua was built in 1838 and has a long tradition of use by Hawaiian royalty. It was in disrepair early in the 1900s and was restored and converted into a museum by the Daughters of Hawai'i in 1927.

Page 84 Fish and poi are the essential foods of a good Hawaiian meal. The fish, akule, is often eaten dried and salted, a flavorful companion to starchy pink-gray poi. When poi, made of cooked taro corm pounded with water, is served thick, as here, it's one-finger poi. Thinner stuff requires more fingers.

Page 85 Colorful outrigger fishing canoes at Ho'okena are often referred to as three-plank canoes for their vertical sides and flat bottoms, although most have a fourth plank at the stern to support an outboard motor.

Pages 86/87 Grotesque images like these at Pu'uhonua O Hōnaunau are called ki'i. Some may represent god figures. Most images of this type were destroyed when the Hawaiian chiefs converted to Christianity.

Pages 88/89 Palms stand like ancient sentinels along the shore at sunset at Pu'uhonua O Hōnaunau.

Pages 90/91 The glow of sunset on Pu'uhonua O Hōnaunau National Historical Park

Page 92 The native Hawaiian sadleria tree fern known as 'ama'u is shorter than the better-known hāpu'u. Early Hawaiians used the starchy interior of the trunk of this fern as food during times of famine.

Page 92 The native Hawaiian goose, or nēnē, is an endangered species whose numbers are being augmented through captive propagation. The regal fowl, seen here at Hawai'i Volcanoes National Park, are the Hawaiian state bird.

Page 93 Dancers turn quickly, sending fiber skirts flying during a Hawaiian ceremony at Kīlauea.

Page 93 A geologist shields himself from the heat as he approaches a skylight over an active lava-tube system, in which lava is flowing from a vent toward the sea.

Page 94 When lava flows in a fluid manner, with a smooth, undulating surface, it is called pāhoehoe. Rough, broken lava is 'a'ā.

Page 94 Lava flows out of a basalt bench into ocean. Much of this quick-cooled rock shatters and becomes sand, feeding black-sand beaches up and down the coast.

Page 95 Palms are reflected in a coastal pool, which is separated from the ocean by a black-sand beach at Punaluʻu.

Page 96 The coconut palms grow thick and strong in the rich volcanic sand of Punaluʻu Black Sand Beach.

Page 97 Leaf capes, feathered kāhili and chanting are part of a traditional ceremony at Halemaʻumaʻu, the firepit within the Kīlauea Caldera.

Page 98 The ʻōhiʻa, growing here among sulfur vents at Hawaiʻi Volcanoes National Park, is one of the first trees to sprout on new lava flows. Its nectar-rich red blossoms provide a source of food for birds and insects, which help bring in more species to populate the new land.

Page 99 Sulfur-rich fumes from deep within the volcano have left yellow crystalline deposits of the mineral on Uwēkahuna Bluff on Kīlauea Volcano.

Page 100 Much of the village and surroundings of Kapoho were destroyed by lava flows from the 1960 eruption of Kīlauea, but the remnants of the quiet coastal community and its rocky bay remain.

Page 101 Olivine crystals are responsible for the name and color of Green Sand Beach, northeast of Ka Lae. The crystals, formed during volcanic eruptions, have eroded out of a cinder cone next to the beach.

Page 102 Lava drips and pours into the sea in a misty sunset scene along the oceanside on the southern slopes of Kīlauea.

Page 103 Lava rises in the cinder cone of Puʻu ʻŌʻō and pours out to form a lava lake.

Page 104 A wave smashes up against the lava flowing into the sea. The continual battle between the land and sea goes back and forth. First the lava gains ground, then the sea undercuts it and causes vast collapses.

Page 105 Much of the volcanic activity at Kīlauea during recent decades has been centered at Puʻu ʻŌʻō, during which the lava sometimes pours out onto the landscapes and infrequently, as shown here, blazes in fountains of fire and rock.

Page 106 When lava flows underground, portions of the overlying rock sometimes cave into the river below, revealing the superheated, incandescent rock below. Such an opening is called a skylight.

Page 107 Lava glows bright orange as it pours out of underground passages onto the seacoast.

Pages 108/109 LAVA(EXPLOSION AT WATER)

Pages 110/111 LAVA INTO OCEAN

Page 112 The southernmost point of the United States is appropriately named South Point in English. Early Hawaiians simply called it Ka Lae, or The Point. The view here is toward the village of Miloliʻi.

Page 113 The region around South Point is one of the most predictably windy in the Islands, and was selected for one of the early Hawaiʻi wind-power programs, the Kamoa Wind Farm.

Pages 114/115 Old coconut palms, their trunks scarred from years of being climbed, rise from the black sand at Punaluʻu.

Pages 116/117 Tree ferns and overhanging *Metrosideros* or ʻōhiʻa trees line the road through Hawaiʻi Volcanoes National Park.

Pages 118/119 A hawksbill turtle rests on the black sand at Punaluʻu Beach. This endangered turtle species nests on only a few beaches in Hawaiʻi, most of them on Hawaiʻi.

Pages 120 Wind across the hot lava whips clouds of steam seaward as rivulets of orange molten rock pour onto coastal shelves.

Pages 121 Lava surrounds the summit of Kīlauea. The structures in the foreground are part of the Hawaiian Volcano Observatory, one of the world's premier sites.

Page 122 Builders of snowmen don't get much time, and often don't have the best snow for building their ephemeral works of art atop Mauna Kea, but they work with what they have.

Page 123 Snow is not rare atop Hawaiʻi's two tallest mountains, whose peaks both rise more than 13,000 feet above sea level, but a thick snow cover is unusual. It draws skiers who enjoy the opportunity Hawaiʻi Island offers to snow-ski and swim at the beach on the same day. Here, Mauna Kea has a thicker mantle of snow than its sister mountain, Mauna Loa, in the background.

Page 124 Snow-capped Mauna Kea oversees the resort area that bears its name: Kaunaʻoa Beach at the Mauna Kea Resort.

Page 125 The Big Island's three tallest peaks, Hualālai with Mauna Kea and Mauna Loa in the background, peek through the clouds that blanket the lower parts of the island.

Pages 126/127 The summit of Mauna Kea is dotted with dozens of cinder cones, most of them barren and arid, lying well above most of Hawaiʻi's weather and substantially higher than the tree line.

Pages 128/129 The Caltech Submillimeter Observatory atop Mauna Kea views the heavens in the electromagnetic spectrum between infrared and short-wavelength radio. This is a frequency range in which viewing from Earth is normally disrupted by the atmosphere. At Mauna Kea, astronomers have found a site that is high enough to be above most of the atmosphere.

Pages 130/131 Snow covers the peak of Mauna Kea in winter. This view looks from the mountain's summit across its cinder cones toward cloud-shrouded Mauna Loa in the distance.

Page 136 Flowers are still regularly laid at the memorial to victims of the April 1, 1946, tsunami that devastated the coastal village of Laupāhoehoe, wiping out the school and killing many of the community's children and teachers.

MEMORIAL TO LAUPĀHOEHOE TIDAL-WAVE VICTIMS